D0819937

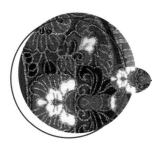

CULTURE
in Japan

Melanie Guile

Raintree
Chicago, Illinois

© 2004 Raintree
Published by Raintree, a division of Reed Elsevier, Inc.
Chicago, Illinois
Customer Service 888-363-4266
Visit our website at www.raintreelibrary.com

All rights reserved. No part of this book may be reproduced or transmitted in any form or by any means, electronic or mechanical, including photocopying, recording, taping, or by any information storage and retrieval system, without permission in writing from the publisher.

For information, address the publisher:
Raintree, 100 N. LaSalle, Suite 1200, Chicago, IL 60602

Printed in China by Wing King Tong.
07 06 05 04 03
10 9 8 7 6 5 4 3 2 1

Library of Congress Cataloging-in-Publication Data
Guile, Melanie.
  Japan / Melanie Guile.
      p. cm. -- (Culture in--)
Includes bibliographical references and index.
  ISBN 1-4109-0470-9 (library binding)
  1. Japan--Civilization--Juvenile literature. I. Title. II. Series:
Guile, Melanie. Culture in-- .
  DS806.G86 2004
  952--dc21

                                    2003008621

Acknowledgments
The publisher would like to thank the following for permission to reproduce photographs:
pp. 6, 24 PhotoDisc; pp. 7, 9, 10, 11, 12, 13, 16, 18, 19, 22, 26, 27, 28, 29B Japan National Tourist Organization; pp. 15, 17 Australian Picture Library; p. 21 Kobal Collection/TOHO; p. 23 Michael Sedunary; p. 25 Sony Australia Limited; p. 29A Coo-ee Picture Library.

Other Acknowledgments
The cover photo of a *Kabuki* actor was supplied by PhotoDisc.

Every effort has been made to contact copyright holders of any material reproduced in this book. Any omissions will be rectified in subsequent printings if notice is given to the publisher.

CONTENTS

Some words are shown in bold, **like this**. You can find out what they mean by looking in the glossary.

CULTURE IN JAPAN

◆ A land apart

Curled like a seahorse off the coasts of Korea and Russia, the islands of Japan lie between the Sea of Japan and the vast Pacific Ocean. Separated from mainland Asia, the Japanese have developed a culture that is very distinct from other Asian countries and cultures.

Legends say that the sun goddess gave birth to the Japanese people at the dawn of time. Some say their ancestors came 2,000 years ago in boats from the islands in the Pacific; others believe they were Chinese invaders. For 2,000 years, these people have made Japan their home, developing their unique way of life. Today Japan's 126 million citizens are extremely proud of their ancient culture and their citizens' many accomplishments.

◆ What is culture?

Culture is a people's way of living. It is the way in which people identify themselves as a group, separate and different from any other. Culture includes a group's language, social customs, and habits, as well as its traditions of art, dance, music, writing, and religion.

Japan's language, writing, arts, and customs have been strongly influenced by its older neighbor, China, but deep in Japanese culture is the drive to be better, faster, and smarter. It is a country of achievers who believe in hard work and are driven by a strong sense of duty.

Even though Japanese culture tends to emphasize group achievement over solitary efforts, the hopes and dreams of individuals are brilliantly expressed in the works of Japan's greatest writers, artists, musicians, filmmakers, and performers. Alongside all of this is a love of beauty and elegance, and a great pride in being Japanese.

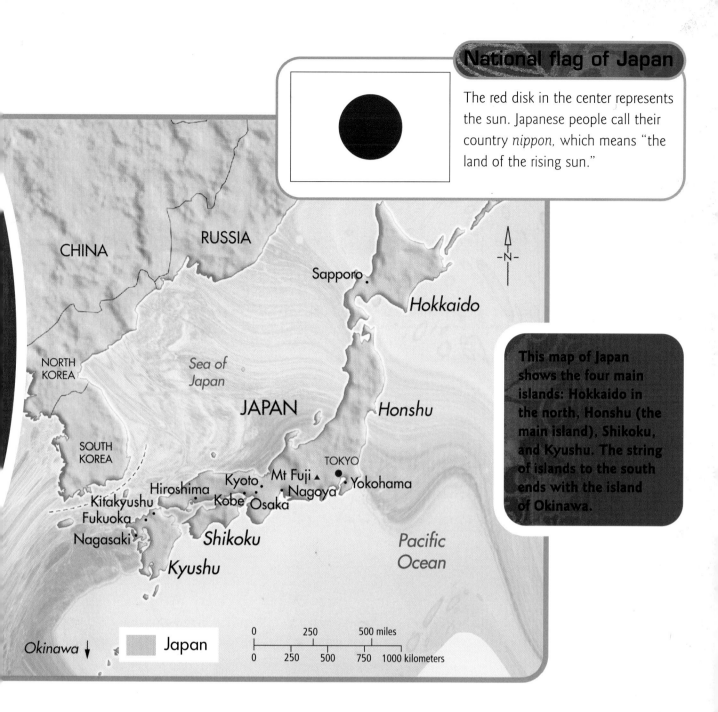

The red disk in the center represents the sun. Japanese people call their country *nippon,* which means "the land of the rising sun."

CHINA

RUSSIA

Sapporo

Hokkaido

NORTH KOREA

Sea of Japan

JAPAN

Honshu

SOUTH KOREA

TOKYO

Kyoto   Mt Fuji ▲   • Yokohama
Hiroshima   Nagoya
Kitakyushu   Kobe Osaka
Fukuoka
Nagasaki

Shikoku

Pacific Ocean

Kyushu

This map of Japan shows the four main islands: Hokkaido in the north, Honshu (the main island), Shikoku, and Kyushu. The string of islands to the south ends with the island of Okinawa.

0   250   500 miles
0   250   500   750   1000 kilometers

Okinawa ↓   Japan

-N-

One culture

To Westerners used to a **multicultural** society, it may seem surprising how many Japanese share the same cultural background. In fact, only one percent of the people living in Japan are not Japanese, and there are laws that make it difficult for foreigners to become Japanese citizens. Although they are known for being generous and friendly to foreign guests, many Japanese want their culture to remain pure and unchanged by outsiders. Being different is generally not encouraged. Minority groups such as the **indigenous** Ainu people still suffer from **discrimination**.

Old and new symbols

The full moon over Mount Fuji, white-faced *geisha* girls in flowery *kimono* robes, **Zen Buddhist** temples where monks meditate—these are the traditional symbols of Japanese culture, but these traditional images represent only a small part of the story.

Today's Japan is fast-moving and competitive. Getting ahead is important and requires dedicating yourself completely to your work, education, or other outside activities. There is no time to **meditate** and little space to be alone. But traditions help to reassure Japanese people that old ways have not died. Crowds still gather under the cherry blossoms every year to celebrate spring. Keeping up the old ways gives the Japanese a connection to the past in a world that is always changing.

Keep cool

Politeness is much more important than telling the blunt truth in Japan. Directly disagreeing with someone is considered bad manners, and getting irritated or angry is definitely unacceptable. Japanese people generally act reserved and prefer not to express strong emotions.

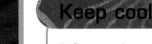

Geisha girls are traditional symbols of Japanese culture.

Today's Japan is fast-paced and competitive.

Times of change

Since their defeat in World War II (1939–1945), the Japanese have shown that they can succeed economically by technical skill and hard work. For decades their country seemed like an economic miracle with full employment and high wages.

However, during the last decade or so, growing problems such as unemployment, homelessness, **terrorism,** and pollution have made many Japanese people reflect on their fast-paced lifestyle. Some question the costs of studying and working so hard. Many aspects of Japanese culture today capture the tension between the drive to live and play hard and the need for peace and rest.

No breaks, thanks

In the past, workers in Japan were not given as many holidays as workers in other countries. It was even considered strange for people to take off all of the days they had earned. This is changing, though, and vacation time in Japan is now comparable to other countries.

7

People often judge performances by the talent and flair of individual directors, actors, or dancers. In Japan performance is not necessarily about **showcasing** individuals. It is often about preserving traditions and achieving perfection in an ancient art.

Kabuki

Kabuki theater is very popular in Japan. It dates back to the early 1600s and involves spectacular stage sets and costumes, music and dancing, and familiar Japanese stories. There is a runway for the actors called a *hanamichi* (flower path) that runs right through the audience.

Action is dramatic and designed to entertain. Performances last all day, meals are brought in, people come and go, and the atmosphere is bustling. *Kabuki* means "song–dance skill," and players must be able to sing, mime, dance, and act. Families of *Kabuki* actors go back centuries, and it is common for players to put a number after their name, representing the generations of performers in their family. Performances are held at the Kabuki Theater and the National Theater, both in Tokyo.

Bugaku

Bugaku is the ancient court dance of Japan and has not changed since about 700 C.E. Several dancers perform slow dance steps accompanied by the traditional *gagaku* orchestra of flutes, strings, and drums. The flowing silk costumes are traditionally either red or green, and the dancers wear hats and white silk slippers, and sometimes masks as well. The aim of the dance is to create a sense of harmony and elegance.

Healing music

The musical accompaniment to *bugaku* is the *gagaku* orchestra. Instruments include the *koto*, a type of thirteen-stringed zither that is 7 feet (2 meters) long; the *biwa*, a short-necked lute; two kinds of flutes; and several drums. The musicians sit on the stage to play and are part of the *bugaku* performance, although the music is also sometimes played on its own. The most famous piece is called *etenraku* ("divine music"). It can take seven years to learn *gagaku*, and the music is said to bring spiritual healing. *Gagaku* is still played at the emperor's court, although most Japanese are more familiar with modern music.

A scene from a *Noh* play provides a glimpse of Japan's oldest form of musical drama.

Noh theater

Noh began around 1300 C.E. in the emperor's court. The language used in performances today dates back to that period. A *Noh* play is not meant to be realistic. Instead, it is more like a ritual that includes storytelling, movement, and mime. Two or three masked actors, plus a chorus of ten singers and four musicians (playing flute and drums), perform before a backdrop of a painted pine tree. One actor watches while the main actor tells of some past event or tragedy.

About 2,000 *Noh* scripts survive, and one of the most famous is *Matsukaze* ("Wind in the Pines") by Kan'ami, written in 1360 C.E. Like Western classical ballet, a *Noh* performance is an elegant and formal kind of stage art. It is much admired by sophisticated audiences in Kyoto and Tokyo.

Puppet theater

Puppet shows are not always just for children. Japan has its own classical puppeteering style dating back to the 1600s. *Bunraku* uses nearly life-sized dolls worked by puppeteers, accompanied by a chanted story and music from a three-stringed lute called a *samisen*. The dolls are very lifelike, and it takes three puppeteers on stage to work each one. The stories are often tragic tales from daily life. One of these is *Keisei Awa no Naruto*, which was written in 1769 and is about a mother and her long-lost daughter. Originally puppeteers passed their skills only to their eldest son, but now nonpuppeteering families and women are welcome in *bunraku*.

Puppeteers perform a *bunraku* play. The name comes from the Osaka puppeteer Uemura Bunrakuken, who revived the art in the 1800s.

Indigenous music

The Ainu are Japan's **indigenous** people of Hokkaido, and their music is distinctive. It uses straw whistles, drums, and flutes. The oldest Ainu music is a type of song called *yukar*, which tells **epic** stories of gods and ancient heroes.

Karaoke is one of the most popular forms of entertainment in Japan.

J-Pop and Western-style music

Pop music is huge in Japan, second only to the United States in CD sales. Japanese pop (called J-Pop) is usually performed by rock bands, such as Hikky and Shonen Knife, as well as by other solo artists (especially young female vocalists), who have star status in Japan. In the last few years, reggae, a style of music from the Caribbean islands, has started to influence music on Okinawa, one of Japan's southernmost islands.

Western-style music in Japan is not all rock and pop. A certain style of songs called *kayookyoku* became popular in the early 1900s. One type of these, called *enka,* were sad ballads. Other types of *kayookyoku* were cheerful, happy tunes. Misora Hibari was a famous *enka* performer who had hit records from the 1940s to the 1980s. Classical music is popular, and the Japan Broadcasting Corporation (NHK) sponsors the famous NHK Symphony Orchestra. Modern music composer Sakamoto Ryuichi won an Academy Award for Best Soundtrack for the film *The Last Emperor* in 1988.

Karaoke

Salarymen (the Japanese word for businesspeople) in Tokyo began the craze for singing the words to pop songs along with backup music. It was their way of letting off tension from the long office week. Today *karaoke* is very popular, and thousands of places offering it are swamped by teens and young adults.

New Year

Long hours of school and work are broken up in Japan with dozens of national and regional festivals. The biggest celebration is *oshoogatsu,* or New Year's, from January 1 to 3. The gods are thanked and welcomed into homes with pine and bamboo decorations on either side of the front door. Over four billion greeting cards are sent to family and friends during each New Year! Children are given gifts of money, and families make their first visit of the year to the **Shinto** shrine or temple to pray for health and safety.

Children

Grandparents often live with the family and look after their grandchildren while the parents work. Very young children are free to play, but once they reach school age, life becomes more competitive, and hard work and self-discipline are expected. Many children have to take a test just to get into kindergarten! "Cram schools" (*juku*) are essential for students to be accepted into the best high schools and universities, and there is a huge amount of pressure at exam time.

Carp-shaped kites decorate houses on Children's Day.

Children's festivals

Several yearly festivals are just for children. *Kodomo-no-hi* on May 5 is Children's Day. Though it was originally just for boys, now girls and boys alike decorate their houses with cloth kites shaped like carp (a type of fish) and eat rice dumplings wrapped in bamboo leaves. The fifth day of the fifth month was traditionally believed to be unlucky, so *Kodomo-no-hi* helped to banish evil spirits and promote good health for children.

Shichi-Go-San (Seven-Five-Three Festival) is for girls of three and seven and boys of three and five. On November 15, the children dress in **kimono** (traditional silk robes) and go to the shrine or temple to offer prayers of thanks for having reached that stage of growth. Parents buy them lollypops called *chitose-ame* ("thousand years candy") for long life.

On March 3, *Ohina-matsuri*, the Doll Festival, is for the health and happiness of little girls. Families display traditionally dressed dolls and decorate the house with peach blossoms, and the girls wear their best *kimono*.

Thousands flock to celebrate spring *hanami* (cherry blossom festival).

Marriage

An average Japanese couple is likely to spend a large amount of money on a wedding ceremony and reception. For many families a family ceremony is held first at a Shinto shrine (nowadays often a room at the reception center). The bride wears a white silk *kimono* and the groom a black one. The priest gives offerings to the Shinto spirits, and the couple drink *sake* (rice wine) while the groom (but not the bride) speaks his vows.

The reception afterward might have 200 guests, including the couple's teachers, bosses, and other important figures. Speeches, songs, and a meal are enjoyed, and the bride appears in several outfits, often including a Western-style wedding dress. Many couples choose to get married overseas because, even including the travel costs, it is cheaper than celebrating at home. Australia and Hawaii are popular choices for Japanese weddings.

The **indigenous** Ainu have an interesting marriage tradition. To propose to a woman, the man comes to her hut with a bowl of cooked rice. He eats half and offers the rest to his sweetheart. If she eats it, she accepts his proposal of marriage. If she puts it to one side, she rejects him.

Cherry blossom time

Thousands of people turn out every weekend in early April to celebrate spring *hanami* (cherry blossom festival). The custom of picnicking under the cherry trees dates back to the 1600s, when poor people gathered for fun and good food outdoors. Today during *hanami*, television news includes a cherry blossom report on the best spots for taking in the beautiful trees.

AINU CULTURE

The Ainu are the **indigenous** people of Japan who live on the northern island of Hokkaido. The Ainu have experienced **discrimination,** but they are fighting to preserve their traditional language and culture.

The people

Traditionally the Ainu (a word that means "human" in the Ainu language) were hunters and gatherers, meaning that they did not live in one place permanently but wandered in search of food. Many Ainu now farm, fish, or work in the tourist trade near Hokkaido's capital city, Sapporo. Village and family life is important to the Ainu, and they have strong spiritual ties with the land, animals, and the natural world. About 25,000 people identify themselves as Ainu, but years of discrimination against them have led many to choose to say that they are Japanese.

Unfortunately, Ainu standards of living, health, and education are generally poorer than those of the majority of Japanese. Organizations such as the Ainu International Network are trying to improve standards. In 1997 the Japanese Parliament finally recognized the cultural rights of the Ainu. They passed an act to promote Ainu culture and spread knowledge of and understanding about Ainu traditions. However, the act does not recognize the Ainus' rights to areas of land that they say were taken from them by the Japanese in the late 1800s.

Owl of ill omen

Beware of the horned owl! The Ainu consider this night-flying hunter a demon, and if one flies above you, bad luck is sure to follow. One remedy is to quickly spit as far as you can to expel the evil. To see an owl fly across the moon also means big trouble. The only way to avoid it is to change your name so that the demon will not know you when it comes.

Dances

To the Ainu, dance is a way of thanking the gods. The *upopo* is a dance performed at the beginning of a celebration, in which women sit in a circle and sing to the beat of drums. *Rimse*, which means "banging sound," is a dance and song to scare away evil spirits after a disaster. Villagers wave swords and stamp their feet as they move from house to house. The *emush rimse* is a kind of sword fight in which two men skillfully duel with each other to a chorus of shouts and encouragement from the audience.

Clothing

Elaborately decorated costumes are worn by the Ainu for dances and special ceremonies. Striking geometric patterns of red, white, black, and blue are sewn onto cloth and made into coats and pants. Traditional clothes were made of bird or fish skins and other natural materials. Fabric called *attush*, made from the bark of elm trees, is still worn. Modern Ainu women wear a kind of bodysuit that is put on over the head as underwear. They wear embroidered headbands as hats, and metal hoop-and-ball earrings. Chunky glass bead necklaces with metal medallions, called *tamasai*, are worn for special occasions.

This indigenous Ainu man is wearing a traditional robe. The Ainu are culturally distinct from the Japanese.

FASHION

A sense of style

Around 800 c.e., when Europeans still wore rough and greasy **homespun** clothes, wealthy Japanese bathed daily and dressed themselves in richly patterned **kimono.** Their sense of style remains today. Japanese fashion designers, such as Yohji Yamamoto, have gained international recognition. Incomes are high in Japan, and a great deal of money is spent on personal appearance.

Tradition with a twist

The elaborate and beautiful *kimono*, Japan's national costume, is still worn at weddings, New Year's, and coming-of-age ceremonies. The *kimono* has twelve parts, including special underwear, layers of silk robes, and the *obi*, a 10-foot-long (3-meter) stiff sash. Thong sandals decorated with silk, called *zori,* and socks with split toes, called *tabi,* are worn, and there are strict rules about how a woman wearing a *kimono* should sit, bow, and walk. A *kimono* can take up to two hours to put on and can cost as much as a small car!

Not surprisingly many modern women and girls are turning away from traditional dress, but designers may be starting a *kimono* revival. New designs include features such as velcro, zippers, and durable fabrics. Lightweight summer *kimono* called *yukata* have been particularly popular. New interpretations include the mini-*yukata*, worn with platform wooden sandals, and a mosquito-proof *yukata*, treated with a chemical to repel summer pests.

The *kimono* is Japan's national dress and is still worn for important occasions.

Ganguro girls show off their platform heels in Tokyo. In 1999 a 23-year-old woman died after falling off of her shoes, and the government issued an official warning against them.

Street wear

Every weekend in Tokyo's Shibuya neighborhood, thousands of teens in wild styles of clothing gather to hang out, be seen, and be photographed. Some of these are *ganguro* girls. Their fantastic outfits began as a protest against old-fashioned Japanese views of women as quiet and modest. The *ganguro* look features micromini skirts, huge platform shoes, brilliant colors, tanned skin with white eyeliner, and bleached or brown-dyed hair often worn in pigtails. Although no two *ganguro* girls look exactly alike, they follow strict dress codes depending on which *ganguro* style they follow. Stores stock this style of clothing under labels such as Bathing Ape and Hysteric Glamour.

Warm inner glow

Short sleeves are "in," but how to stay both warm and fashionable in Japan's freezing winters? Japanese scientists have come up with high-tech underwear. New fabrics contain ceramic particles that give off **infrared** radiation to keep the wearer warm.

FOOD

Like many aspects of Japanese culture, pleasing harmony, or *wa,* is the key to cuisine in Japan. Traditionally, Japanese food must have three features: it should look beautiful, be attractively presented, and, of course, taste good. Ingredients are fresh, lightly cooked or raw, and barely spiced so that the pure taste of the food comes through. Traditional foods are rice, seafood, vegetables, seaweed, and soybeans, but today every kind of international food is available in Japan.

Rice

In the Japanese language, the word for "meal" is *gohan*, which means "rice" (just as we might say "daily bread"). At one time rice was a form of currency, and **samurai** warriors were paid with it. Bowls of rice are offered to the dead at **Shinto** religious festivals, and *sake* (rice wine) is drunk on special occasions. Some scholars believe that the cooperation between farmers that was necessary to grow rice gave rise to the strong group loyalty that characterizes the modern Japanese. However, statistics show that Japanese people are eating less rice today. Japan now imports billions of dollars in food every year, but all the rice it needs is still grown by its own farmers.

Visual appeal is important in Japanese cuisine, as shown by this *sushi* platter.

Fast food

Pizza and sandwiches are popular choices for a quick lunch, or you can pop out for a *Mosburger*, a popular hamburger, at one of the thousands of hamburger and other food outlets in Japan's crowded and busy cities. Beautifully packed lunch boxes called *bento* offer students and workers a ready-made carry-out meal. Cans of hot coffee, milky, strong, and very sweet, can be bought at vending machines. Every train station has fast-food outlets to serve **commuters**. Businesspeople might grab a quick meal of noodles late at night on their way home from the office.

In Japanese cities it is common to see plastic models of dishes placed in cases outside restaurants to help diners make their choices.

Eating out

In Japan restaurants tend to specialize in one kind of food. Noodle bars serve *soba*, which are thin, brown buckwheat noodles served in a fish broth. You can have them plain with a dipping sauce or in many other ways. A combination with tofu, spring onions, or a raw egg is called *tsukimi soba*, which means "moon-gazing." *Udon* is similar to *soba*, but these noodles are made from wheat and are thick and white. *Sushi* bars sell beautifully prepared morsels of rice and fish wrapped in seaweed. *Sashimi* is a popular meal consisting of strips of raw fish served with soy sauce and *wasabi* (a hot greenish horseradish).

Forbidden food

Eating red meat was forbidden in Japan until 1867, when Emperor Meiji opened up the country to foreign influences. Today most older Japanese still prefer white meat or seafood, although Kobe beef is an expensive delicacy. However, younger Japanese frequently enjoy burgers made from Australian and U.S. beef.

School and work are demanding in Japan, so videos and television are generally considered light escapes from the grind of daily life. Nonetheless many Japanese film directors are highly regarded by serious **critics.**

Early films

Japanese filmmakers produced their first film in 1898. Popular silent movie themes were the deeds of *samurai* warriors and heroes. Instead of subtitles, actors were hired to speak words to go along with the silent action. During World War II, the Japanese miliary used films with sound for **propaganda,** but after the war, films began to attract attention as an art form.

Golden age of film

Three brilliant movie directors established the golden age of Japanese film in the 1950s. Kenji Mizoguchi (1898–1956) trained as an artist, which shows in his beautiful **cinematography.** His intense film *The Life of Oharu* is about one woman's tragic life, and it won international praise. The films of Yasujiro Ozu (1903–1963) focus on ordinary Japanese working people and the **suppression** of true feelings. His famous *Tokyo Story* (1953) is often rated among the ten best movies ever made.

Akira Kurosawa's (1910–1998) career spanned almost 50 years. Known for his spectacular cinematography, funny and moving plots, and great characters, Kurosawa's films have been copied around the world. *Rashomon* (1950), which is about an attack on a woman told from four different viewpoints, won first prize at the Venice Film Festival. His 1954 film *Shichinin-no-Samurai* (*The Seven Samurai*) is about a group of warriors who save a small village from bandits, and is one of the most admired works in film history. The successful 1960 Hollywood movie *The Magnificent Seven* is a remake of it.

Reality TV

Japan's reality TV show "Sata Suma" sends a "maid" to selected viewers' homes to surprise busy families and do the morning's housework. The maid's cheery greeting *"oh-ha!"* is short for *ohayo gozaimasu* (good morning), and it has become the latest way to greet friends at school. But the maid is actually a man. He is 23-year-old pop star Shingo Katori of the pop group SMAP. The show is so popular that *oh-ha* was awarded a government prize for "trendy word of 2000," and the Minister of Education invited Shingo to help promote a campaign to encourage communication within families.

A scene from the film *The Seven Samurai* (*Shichinin-no-Samurai*), directed by Akira Kurosawa

The new generation

Television and video devastated filmmaking in Japan. From a peak audience of 1.1 billion in 1958, movies now attract about 120 million viewers a year. But a new wave of movie directors is fighting back. Takeshi Kitano (known as "Beat" Takeshi) is the biggest media personality in Japan. He has eight television programs a week, and regular radio and newspaper features. He began his career as a stand–up comedian in the 1970s, but now writes, directs, and acts in his own films. *Sonatine* (1993) won praise at the Cannes Film Festival, but his most famous movie is *Hana Bi* (*Fireworks*) (1997), which is about two police detectives and what happens after a shootout.

Itami Juzo (1933–1997) began his career as an actor and then turned to directing. His comedies like *Marusa no Onna* (*A Taxing Woman*) show the social and political quirks of modern Japan.

Animated praise

Animated movies **(anime)** make up one-third of all box office sales in Japan. *Spirited Away* (2002), by Hayao Miyazaki, is an exciting, heartwarming story about a little girl who stumbles into a magical spirit realm. Critics around the world praised the film for taking animation to a new level of excellence.

BOOKS,
Poetry, and Comics

Japan has the highest **literacy** rate in the world—almost 100 percent of the population can read and write. The Japanese are avid readers of books, newspapers, magazines, and *manga* (comics), and they have a long tradition of fine literature.

Classic literature

The Tale of Genji by Lady Murasaki Shikibu was written around 1000 C.E. It is a story of life, love, and secret plotting at the Emperor's court, and is regarded as Japan's greatest classic. A much-loved travel book by the poet Matsuo Basho (1644–1694) is *The Narrow Road to the Deep North*. Modern fans of this book still climb the three mountain peaks it describes. One of Japan's greatest modern writers is Natsume Soseki (1867–1916). He was a lecturer in English at Tokyo University in the early 1900s, but gave up his job to write. One of his more famous novels is *Kokoro* (meaning "feelings" or "the heart"). Written in 1914, it is a sad story about loneliness and betrayal. Kawabata Yasunari (1899–1972), who wrote the famous story *Snow Country*, won the Nobel Prize for literature in 1948.

Haiku

Japanese culture values simplicity and subtlety, and the *haiku* form of poetry expresses both. In just seventeen **syllables,** the writer tries to express deep emotions, often about the beauty of nature. The moon, falling cherry blossoms, and snowy Mount Fuji are popular subjects.

The Japanese writer Natsume Soseki appears on the 1,000-yen banknote (worth about 84 cents).

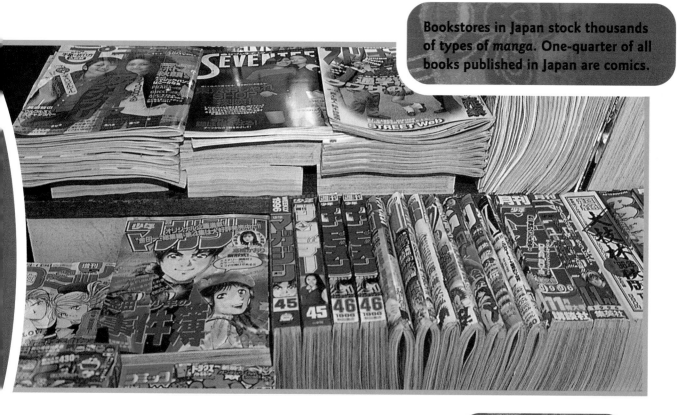

Bookstores in Japan stock thousands of types of *manga*. One-quarter of all books published in Japan are comics.

Mad about *manga*

Manga (which means "playful pictures") is the Japanese word for comics. Japanese people read more *manga* than any other country in the world. In Japan there are special comics for teenagers *(shonenshi)*, for young adults *(yangushi)*, and even for businesspeople. *Manga* are like films or novels, with complex story lines and characters. Japanese *manga* artists are famous for their skill and inventiveness, and they are treated like pop stars. Over six million *manga* are read every week. The most popular is *Shonen Jump*, which is now sold in English in the United States.

Father of Japanese manga

The first comics appeared in Japan around 700 C.E., but they only took off after World War II in 1945. The man responsible for their popularity is Japan's greatest *manga* artist, Tezuka Osamu (1926–1989). He was inspired by Walt Disney and saw the animated film *Bambi* 80 times! Tezuka created the world-famous characters Astro Boy (*Tetsuwan Atomu*) in 1963 and Kimba the White Lion in 1965. He drew 150,000 comic strips in his lifetime and started the modern craze for comics and **anime** in Japan. A museum in Osaka is dedicated to Tezuka.

Millions of newspapers

More than 50 million newspapers are sold daily in Japan. With over ten million readers, the daily *Yomiuri Shimbun* has the largest circulation of any daily paper in the world.

Fads

Fads come and go in Japan, especially among teenagers and kids. While older people value Japan's ancient traditions, young people go crazy for anything new and different. One in three Japanese owns a cell phone, and young people treat them like fashion accessories. There are even cell-phone receivers shaped like shoes, and ballpoint pens or teddy bears that flash or move when a call is received.

A new kind of candy called "365 Days Birthday Teddy" has become popular in Japan. Inside every box of chocolate is a small, brightly colored bear—each one marked with its own birthday, a different one for every day of the year. Naturally collectors want to get the bear with their own birth date, but there is no way of knowing the date until you open the box. The demand for the chocolate treats is so great that manufacturers cannot keep up.

High-tech toys

Japan is a leader in high-tech goods, so it is no surprise that some of the most popular electronic games were invented by the Japanese. Nintendo of Kyoto launched its first home video game system in 1985. It became an instant success. Nearly twenty years later, the games are more powerful and complex, but the action-adventure formula is the same.

The introduction of games featuring the Pokémon characters extended the fame of Nintendo. More than 250 cute creatures appear in the video games, as well as on trading cards and in cartoons. Popular characters, such as Pikachu, are beloved by kids all over Japan and around the world.

Like children everywhere, Japanese kids love anything new and different. Recent fads include electronic games and toys and an ancient Chinese board game.

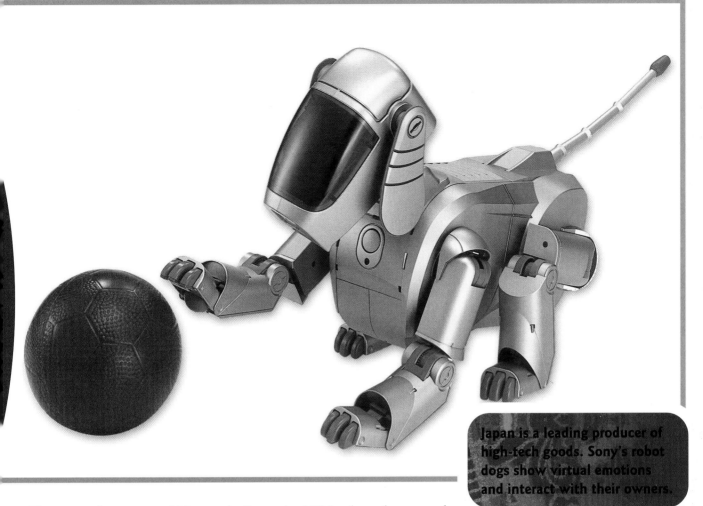

Japan is a leading producer of high-tech goods. Sony's robot dogs show virtual emotions and interact with their owners.

The craze for *tamagotchi* began in Japan in 1996 when the toymaker Bandai Company created **virtual** toys. These egg-shaped electronic gadgets fit in the palm of the hand and were programmed to behave like living pets, demanding food, sleep, or affection. Children were so distracted by their *tamagotchi* that they could not concentrate on their studies, and schools banned them. Updated versions include robots that show emotions and **interact** realistically with their owners.

Go

Go is an ancient Chinese board game for two using black and white stones on a wooden board. Usually played by older people, *go* has taken off among schoolchildren. The reason is a *manga* comic strip in the magazine *Shonen Jump*. In one of its story lines, called *Hikaru no go*, a boy named Hikaru learns to play the game from a phantom *go* master. In 2000 the Japan *Go* Association had 16,000 school children turn up at its annual *go* competition and had to turn hundreds away.

School rules

Japanese students are expected to clean their schools (even the toilets) every day. Teachers are strict and expect no talking in class. Extracurricular clubs are popular for sports and art activities, so sometimes kids spend as many as twelve hours a day at school!

ARTS AND CRAFTS

The Japanese have developed an artistic style that is simple yet beautiful. Some say that this reflects the influence of **Zen Buddhism,** a religion that emphasizes simplicity and inner calm. Understated elegance is certainly admired above showy extravagance. This can be seen in everyday things like the intricately carved radish flowers at a *sushi* bar or the quiet beauty of a temple rock garden in Kyoto.

Master potters are honored in Japan as "living national treasures."

Painting

Painting has always been popular in Japan. Clear open spaces, tiny details, and simple subjects like flowers, birds, and landscapes are typical of Japanese paintings. Until the 1900s the Japanese wrote with a brush, so ink painting was a common art form. Early pictures show a strong Chinese influence, but around 1600 C.E. a unique style emerged, with gold-leaf backgrounds and rich colors painted on folding screens. Wall hangings often showed scenes from royal court life.

Woodblock prints

In the 1600s, only noblemen could afford original paintings. However, the development of woodblock printing meant that pictures could be printed cheaply, and so *ukiyo-e* (woodcut prints) became popular. Each image was first drawn on tracing paper by the artist. The engraver then carved the image in raised **relief** onto a block of wood. Finally the printer covered the block with ink and then pressed paper over it to produce the picture. Subjects were often people having fun in the entertainment area of old Edo (today's Tokyo). Many woodblock prints were pictures of *Kabuki* actors, similar to today's posters of rock stars. *Ukiyo-e* means "floating world," named after the **frivolous** subjects represented. These prints were not treated as precious at the time; they were enjoyed, then thrown away or used as wrapping paper. Today *ukiyo-e* sell for huge prices at art auctions.

China and pottery

An artist adds a pattern to a bowl.

Japanese pottery is world famous, and the designs, shapes, and finishes are beautiful. The word for pottery is *setomono* after the town Seto, where the first **kiln** operated in 1242 C.E. Kyoto is the center for the famous *raku-yaki* designs. *Raku* means "enjoy," and this character (word) appears as decoration on special bowls made for serving tea. Finer, lighter porcelain came to Japan from Korea in 1598. It was exported to Europe for more than 100 years before Europeans discovered how to make it. Distinctive finishes include a white crackle glaze and a rich red and black lacquer. Master potters today are honored in Japan as "living national treasures."

Home decorating

Underground at Shinjuku Station in Tokyo, office workers rush past makeshift cardboard shacks where homeless men live. Unemployment was unknown in Japan until the 1990s, when joblessness left former salarymen with nowhere else to live. There is no **social security** in Japan, and people can easily fall on very hard times. Resisting police attempts to remove them in 1995, the homeless men painted vivid murals on their cardboard house walls. A master artist named Yamamura supervises and coordinates dozens of paintings on the cardboard-box homes. Now the public and critics have taken notice and are opposing further attempts to remove the artists.

The art of living things

In Japan people have a great love of nature. Because many Japanese could never afford a private garden, many forms of art aim to bring the spirit and peace of nature indoors.

The ancient art of *bonsai* involves growing miniature trees. Saplings are shaped with wire and pruned to look as if they are fully grown. They are planted in shallow pots to stunt their growth and show off their roots and branches. *Bonsai* trees can last for hundreds of years.

Ikebana developed in the 1400s as a way for **samurai** warriors to learn patience, tolerance, and love of nature through arranging flowers. The aim is to produce a pleasing harmony between the flowers, the container, and the setting. Withered branches, seed pods, and fruit are used as well as blooms. There are strict rules about how each arrangement should look, and different *ikebana* styles flourish in Japan and throughout the world.

The art of *ikebana* uses plants and flowers to bring the form and beauty of nature indoors.

The Japanese have been gardening for centuries. In the **Zen Buddhist** religion, gardens are valued as places for **meditation** and for finding inner peace. There are three main types of Japanese garden: *tsukiyama*, a hilly garden with water ponds and bridges; *chaniwa*, a garden that surrounds a traditional tea house; and *kare-sansui*, which means "dry riverbed" and is a remarkable stone and raked sand garden that has no plants at all. The most famous *kare-sansui* is the walled garden of the Ryoan-ji Temple in Kyoto, created in 1499. Its fifteen large rocks are placed so that no matter how you view them, one of the rocks is always hidden.

Body art

In the West tattoos are not normally regarded as art. However, in Japan, the ancient Japanese form of body art (*irezumi*) uses the whole body as a canvas. Designs are large and flowing, with light colors and a great deal of detail. Popular themes include tigers, flowers, folk heroes, dragons for happiness, and the *koi* carp, the fish that is a traditional symbol of courage and success. The tattoos are applied by hand using vegetable dyes and soot, and they take from one to ten years to complete!

Modern Western-style tattoos are applied by machine and often use images from popular culture, such as Disney characters. Because they normally cover a small part of the body, they are called *wan-pointo* (one-point). *Wan-pointo* tattoos are generally looked down upon by the tattoo masters.

Traditional Japanese tattoos called *irezumi* cover the body from neck to knees and take up to ten years to complete.

Children on field trips often visit the garden of the Ryoan-ji Temple and try to figure out how to see all fifteen rocks at once.

Prince of the knitting world

Hand-knitting has become popular thanks to knitwear designer and instructor Mitsuharu Hirose. This celebrity hand-knits and models his own garments, runs his own TV show and fashion magazines, and gets floods of fan letters. To people who think men should leave the knitting to women, Mitsuharu Hirose says, "Being different is all right."

GLOSSARY

anime type of Japanese animation

cinematography art of filming movies

commuter person who travels daily to and from work

critic person who gives an opinion to the public about something that has been created, usually a work of art

discrimination act of treating people unfairly on the basis of their race, gender, or religion, or for any other reason

epic long poem about the adventures of a hero

fad fashion or craze that only lasts for a short time

frivolous not serious

geisha female Japanese entertainer who is trained in singing, dancing, playing music, and lively conversation

homespun rough handmade fabric

indigenous original or native to a particular country or area

infrared type of invisible light that supplies warmth

interact to have an active relationship with another thing or person

kiln very hot oven used for making pottery

kimono silk wraparound robe that is the traditional costume for women in Japan

literacy ability to read and write

meditate to rest the mind through relaxation techniques such as sitting quietly and breathing calmly

meditation act of meditating

multicultural made up of people from many different races and cultures

propaganda materials (such as posters, brochures, or movies) that promote a set of beliefs or ideas to the public

relief image or pattern that is raised up from a surrounding flat surface

samurai highly trained Japanese warrior

Shinto Japanese religion in which followers worship the spirits of nature and the spirits of their own ancestors

showcasing showing off

social security system by which a government provides money to support elderly people who no longer work or people who have lost their jobs

suppression practice of silencing emotions or opinions that are considered unacceptable

syllable individual part of a word that has a separate sound when the word is spoken aloud

terrorism deliberate use of violence against innocent people to inspire fear for political purposes

virtual almost exactly like reality. This word often refers to the lifelike experiences created by computers.

Zen Buddhist follower of, or having to do with, a form of Buddhism that is common in Japan and is known for its emphasis on meditation. Buddhists follow the teachings of a holy man, Gautama Buddha (who lived from about 563 B.C.E. to 483 B.C.E.), and strive for a peaceful state called enlightenment.

FURTHER
Reading

Behnke, Alison. *Japan in Pictures.* Minneapolis: Lerner, 2002.

Hamanaka, Sheila, and Ayano Ohmi. *In Search of the Spirit: The Living National Treasures of Japan.* Illustrated by Sheila Hamanaka. New York: HarperCollins, 1999.

Khanduri, Kamini. *Japanese Art and Culture.* Chicago: Raintree, 2004.

Lansford, Lewis, and Chris Schwarz. *The Changing Face of Japan.* Chicago: Raintree, 2003.

Poisson, Barbara Aoki. *The Ainu of Japan.* Minneapolis: Lerner, 2002.

Shelley, Rex. *Japan.* Tarrytown, N.Y.: Marshall Cavendish, 2001.

INDEX